Copyright 2019 Rex "Mick" Lentz
All rights reserved.
ISBN: 9781698810195

Putting Aside Humility
For God's sake

Spring/Summer 2019

Rex "Mick" Lentz

Also by Mick Lentz

Some Knots in the Prayer Rug
    Selected Poems from the 70s and 80s

Tying the Fringe Knots
    Collected Poems 2010-2014

At the Victory Party
    Collected Poems 2015-2017

"words fly, written things remain"
Fournier

"literature is orchestrated platitudes"
Thornton Wilder

Estragon: "I can't go on like this"
Vladimir: "That's what you think"
Samuel Beckett
Waiting for Godot

"The scholar, where ever he resides, is grave, as if he were apprehensive of difficulties"
Confucius

Tim Liz Diana Mike Jim Denny Gail

    valued friends trusted friends
    good in a pinch friends
    tolerant of eccentricity
    knowledgeable in the life skills
    friends who find comfort in their friends
    friends that allow me to share their journey

my inestimable gratitude for
Cover and art design by Jim McClear
Editing and formatting by Diana Lentz

Content

I woke up under an MG 1
Once a pleasure was found 3
Working to ascertain 5
I acknowledge this day 7
I scan my horizon 9
What a pleasure it has been 11
A round thing seems 13
As I fell 15
The craft of writing 17
I hobbled into a hospital 19
Peril is my name 21
A peculium 23
I think of the first time 25
Burdened with knowledge 27
I endeavor 29
Always start with once 31
In April 33
No 35
Main character 37
Perhaps now 39
I must have in my time 41
I bought 43
Sun gonna shine 45
No way around it 47
Favor me 49

I woke up under a flipped MG
with only a grass stain on my forehead

I have fallen off tractors in front of
deadly implements and escaped harm

I put my deer rifle down safety off
and it fired just past my head

I was once known as one of Ann Arbor's most
dependable impaired drivers and was always
nominated to take the wheel for home

so many times calamity must have
awaited around a corner not taken

I have missed more than I found presumably
to have now taken my place in l'ancien régime

once a pleasure was found
there was a rush to pile on

once a nibble was provocative
once a mound was sacred

once we were observant
in our subservience

once victims of historical convention
now we suffer the ironies of freedom

working to ascertain if when or which things are
believable while living in this cloud of uncertainty
has always seemed the only inevitable pursuit

so after an honest life long effort in that regard my preferred
accommodation to approaching death would be to plan
decomposition in that linen suit impregnated with those
mushroom spores   a most efficient modality

January 2019

I acknowledge this day with Gail
as we continue our walk together
how do I share my appreciation

I would sashay along with her for an everlasting day
with every up and down the angle of her hips still delight
her presence still expiates my timid approach to life

February 2019

I scan my horizon
I look over my vista
I question its veracity

I suspect that the anxious muttering
I hear in the gravity waves is because
the self-aware were not invited

February 2019

what a pleasure it has been
        mostly
just to have been in a reality

I circle in amazed wonderment
in an orbit that is within another orbit
around another orbit then around another

approaching any further toward the
final picture would undermine my balance
and imply there might be an end to the mystery

February 2019

a round thing seems in
contrast to a square thing

very hugely big may seem at
the far end of the unimaginably small

that we are sized exactly
in the middle of the universal scale
must mean something

perhaps center court on the spectrum
is what allows the imaginary to solidify

as I fell I prospected for a landing space
I aimed for a snow bank rolling on my left shoulder
that would be the least injurious

in flight as I positioned myself
I thought of coach Holland
teaching by repetition how to roll
when you hit the ground

on my subsequent fall
I was on the ground so fast
I thought time snatched back
what I had stolen from her in the previous event

February 2019

the craft of writing
a sticky wicket or a gushing exuberance

Red Smith said 'twas easy
just sit at a typewriter and open a vein

was it Kafka whose hero spent
five years on the first paragraph of his novel

didn't Capote say Kerouac was a typist not a writer

I place words along an unnoticed
vine that blossoms only occasionally with
little promise of any future glory

the abjection of criticism is thus avoided
at the expense of community with likeminded fools

I hobbled into a hospital with a pain
a striking list of protocols propelled me into its bowels
everyone but me knew what to do

they all popped in and out with collegial approbations
I tried with all the charm I could muster to be
likeable but they had seen that trick before

underneath all the civility a chess match
of inquisition and probing along with
the surrender of my modesty and liberty

my aim was to go home
theirs was to follow the dictates
proscribed for my condition

a truce of sorts prevailed
they decided I was rational
I decided that they had my interests at heart

recovery was testing which drugs had
the least toxic effects and practicing how
I might get along on the outside

I was not ready to die quite yet
so I was pleased they all set me up
for some more time in my life

a couple more years sounds pretty good
it will have to look much bleaker than this to
present a valid reason to consider a self-imposed departure

March 2019

peril is the name
it stands at your side simmering in danger
you are listening to it call

we sense some distemper in life
bad shit does seem to happen

we are nothing but ash that has
fallen through the grates of the solar furnace

we have nothing much to be proud of
other than our ardent
desire for self-preservation

March 2019

A peculium, a mesne lord, a feudatory and a republican operative walk into a bar. The inevitable conversation occurs. Being the front man for a ruling class, shilling for their overlords, entailed a price few were willing to pay but for that few willing to surrender their morality for social elevation it was an entrance into the higher social classes.
It would be manageable save for the inevitable over reach and greed of their superiors. There will always be a point at which their power is unsustainable due to the loss of perspective.
They never seem happy with enough.

I think of the first time I did a thing
when I consider the last time as it now approaches

just now I am examining the filigree my personal
stamp has put around the arc of my covenants

I have a perch now that was
problematic in my earlier years

now I can gaze across the pleasantries
and steer clear of the desultory

burdened with knowledge
subsumed in rivers of experience

I wade out into the shallows of my rectitude
and cut a foot on the sharpness of my perceptions

that opening is invaded by opportunists
a feverish exposure of my shortcomings results

I endeavor to relieve my dismay
and release the stains of yesterday
I have misbehaved in grand fashion

though I feel pressed to examine and
enumerate my malfeasance in detail
any search for absolution could not expect forgiveness

though my demise is fixing to come by soon
there may still be time to try confession as a purge of burden
though by now it is of such laughably little consequence

April 2019

always start with once
    walking into a bar
    a dense wood
    a trench in WWI

then remark on surroundings
then observe a querulous proposal

then allow there is trouble when words
stumble conveying what the eyes see

April 2019

in april spring is a rising
of photonic energy

when the time comes
got to get busy

this period of the cycle
has lots of clever excitements

with a seductive appeal that arouses
in me a desire to press on with the day

no measure of compassion
could be restitution for our lonely position as
the only self-aware beings in the known universe

we are such a crisp definition of anomaly
such is our sorrow and our pride
such is our first and only sin

May 2019

main character
>   crazy love
>   gimme love love love love
>   crazy love

chorus replies
>   no such thing as love
>   no such thing

main character
>   I disagree
>   it is my choice to love
>   even in the face of problematic rationales

chorus
>   convenience and hormones
>   answer every question

main character
>   and yet I persist
>   in thinking otherwise

May 2019

perhaps now but think back
did our theology really go too far

take this in remembrance of me
      it then turns into blood and flesh

a Christ is born
      must be from a virgin

a crucifixion then the tomb
      he has risen from the dead

all this increased our control of the masses
how could there be a hell without miracles

it was left to us to manage our transition to human
what would you have had us do

I must have in my time amused
Calliope and Erata with my antics

I did offer proper abasement and reverence

all nine sisters may offer us
answers to questions not asked

a message will arrive that
we will transcribe and call our own

it seems to me that in a multiverse there
is room for such a panoply of charmingly
undependable well wishers

I bought "Preface to a 20 Volume Suicide Note" at Paperbacks Unlimited in Highland Park Michigan in 1966. It quickened my heart to discover someone whose writing drew me in and somehow molded my aesthetic in a certain way that though lost or subsumed at times remained my perspective as other influences took root.
I remember how clearly he spoke. He brought me to life through his eyes.
I know LeRoi Jones was his slave name but it has nostalgic resonance for me.
I make this note to acknowledge that for me he opened the largest door in the universe.

May 2019

sun gonna shine in
my backdoor some day

so I always thought in the darker days
a strict application of probability told me so

to my chagrin the coin can
land many times in a row on tails

the number of places π has been calculated reminds
me one can still and always hope for a clarifying outcome

May 2019

no way around it
I am in a sort of heaven as I write

not anything approaching perfect
but allowing pleasures where none should be

there seems to be a sympathetic other
dimensional shoulder upon which to
ameliorate our sorrows at times

but tonight I ascribe it to
Respighi's ancient airs and dances
Kirk Vonnegut
and a fair amount of sleep the night before

May 2019

favor me with acknowledgement oh ineffable one
anoint me with the wisdom beyond time and space
allow me passage oh silent one
a way through to the glory

a remembrance not dependent on the living

May 2019

Made in the USA
Middletown, DE
23 January 2024

48030971R00040